EXPLORING NATURE

JOURNAL FOR KIDS

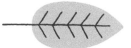

OBSERVE AND RECORD THE OUTDOORS

KIM ANDREWS

ROCKRIDGE
PRESS

Letter to
PARENTS AND TEACHERS

Hello parents, teachers, and mentors! Introducing kids to nature journaling is a great way to get them outside and learning in a natural environment.

When children observe nature, they get physical exercise and fresh air while also studying science, practicing art, and reinforcing their writing skills as they document what they see.

With this book, your child or student will learn to observe, draw, document, ask questions about, and research what they see outside. Have your child read through each section in part 1 before they begin journaling, or read through it with them. Study our journaling tips, and put them into practice with our writing prompts. Once you reach part 2, your child will be ready to journal on their own. If you are looking for more ways to learn about and enjoy nature, this journal's companion book, *The Nature Activity Book for Kids*, is full of fun facts and activities that go along with the sections found in this journal.

Most importantly, thank you for seeing the value in nature and outdoor learning. The more we teach children about our world, the more likely they are to take care of it and protect it. I sincerely hope this journal renews your child's sense of wonder, sparks their creativity, and brings knowledge and joy into their life.

EXPLORING NATURE
JOURNAL FOR KIDS

Interior and Cover Designer: Kristine Brogno
Art Producer: Sue Bischofberger
Editor: Katharine Moore
Production Editor: Erum Khan
Illustrations © Katy Dockrill, 2019
ISBN: Print 978-1-64152-363-9

Letter to KIDS

Nature is full of so many magical things to see. Nature journaling will teach you to slow down and start seeing that magic! Perhaps you will begin to notice leaves spinning down from a tree, fairy rings of mushrooms growing in the woods, or a glistening spiderweb on a dewy morning.

A nature journal is a fun way to keep track of the many strange and wonderful things found in our world. You will learn to observe nature closely, take notes on what you see, and even practice your drawing skills. Your journal is a place where you can experiment with new skills and get creative! Journaling is a fun way to learn and enjoy time in nature. While you are exploring, I hope you make many friends, learn the names of a few new plants and animals, experiment with drawing, and make memories that last a lifetime!

SAFETY FIRST

Spending time in nature is great fun, but always keep an eye out for the following hazards.

LEAVES OF THREE
Let it be

Poison OAK   Poison IVY

POISON OAK AND POISON IVY:

Avoid these plants or you may get an itchy rash. You can recognize these plants by their clusters of three leaves: Remember the old saying, "Leaves of three, let it be."

Honey Bee HIVE

BEEHIVES: Bees are busy making honey. Stay back or you may get stung!

WASP AND HORNET NESTS: Wasps and hornets are protective of their homes, and have a painful sting.

Hornet NEST

SNAKES: Stay away from woodpiles and long grass where venomous snakes could be hiding.

Snakes

FIRE ANT MOUNDS: Avoid standing on these anthills. Fire ants bite and then sting!

Fire Ant HILLS

WILD ANIMAL HOMES: Use caution when exploring caves and large holes, because an animal could be living inside.

UNIDENTIFIED BERRIES AND MUSHROOMS: Some berries and mushrooms are edible, but many are poisonous. Always check with an adult!

Unidentified BERRIES

Unidentified MUSHROOMS

TICKS AND MOSQUITOES: Ticks and mosquitoes can carry diseases. Especially during warm months, wear bug spray and check yourself for ticks after playing outside.

Ticks

DEEP, FAST-MOVING WATER: Always have an adult nearby when exploring bodies of water.

Fast WATER

Part 1

THE EXPLORER'S TOOLKIT

Keeping a journal is an important part of observing nature. This first section will explain what a nature journal is, give you helpful tips and ideas to try, and provide you with space to practice the skills you learn.

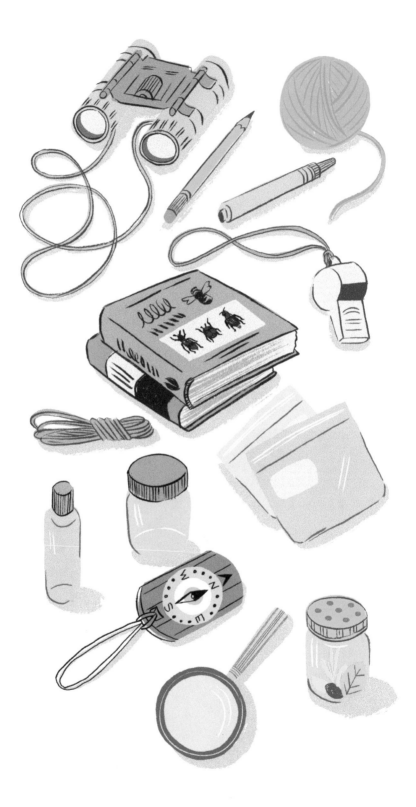

WHAT'S A NATURE JOURNAL?

A nature journal is your own private collection of notes, thoughts, ideas, and drawings about what you observe outside. You can organize and decorate your journal however you'd like: Add real photographs, poetry, pressed flowers, feathers, stamps, and other embellishments, or keep it simple with just words and drawings.

Either way, it's good to start by learning the basics of observing, drawing, and note taking. Ask yourself these two questions: What in nature am I curious about? And, what in nature excites me?

To give you an example of how a journal works, here's a sample page from a morning of bird-watching. I like to include the date, location, and weather at the top. "My Field Notes" is where I jot down my impressions while I'm outside, and "Looking Back" is where I write up my thoughts and research later on, when I have time to look everything over.

MAY 12, 2019, 2:00 P.M.

FRONT YARD OF MY HOUSE

SUNNY AND WARM (75 DEGREES F)

MY FIELD NOTES

-NEST IN HOLLY BUSH

-3 FUZZY BABY BIRDS IN NEST

-BRIGHT RED NORTHERN CARDINAL SWOOPED IN TO SCARE ME OFF

-BIRDS EAT THE BERRIES FROM THE BUSH

LOOKING BACK

I LEARNED THAT THE MALE CARDINAL IS PROTECTIVE OF THE NEST. FURTHER RESEARCH TAUGHT ME THAT THE FEMALE CREATES THE NEST ON HER OWN, AND THEN BOTH THE MALE AND FEMALE CARDINALS FEED AND TAKE CARE OF THE NEW BABIES ONCE THEY HATCH.

Berries

Feather

Seedpod

Northern
Cardinal

LOOK AROUND YOU

The first step in nature journaling is to become a noticer. As a noticer, you will learn to see the everyday things that most people miss. Here are some tips to get you started.

Stay still and quiet. If birds, squirrels, and other small animals don't notice you, they will be more likely to come close, giving you a better view.

Start observing from the ground up! Focus your eyes on the ground around you. Begin to look up, noticing what you see around you until your eyes reach the sky.

Choose one thing to focus on. Take a closer look at something you're curious about or that you find exciting.

Use your senses. Pay attention not only to what you see but also to what you hear and smell. You can use your sense of touch to help describe the feeling of tree bark, rocks, moss, and some plants. Be extra careful not to touch poisonous plants, and never taste wild berries, mushrooms, or other plants without a trained plant expert's advice.

Use these journal prompts to practice this method of observing things around you. You'll be amazed at what you start to notice!

Luna Moth

Giant Walking Stick

1. Sit or lie on the ground (watch for ant hills!). Do you notice any insects, green moss, smooth stones, colorful mushrooms, four-leaf clovers, or anything else that catches your eye? Describe what you see here:

_____

_____

_____

2. Take a five-minute sensory walk. Slip off your shoes and walk on different textures, like grass, moss, rocks, dirt, sand, and so on. Pay close attention to what you see, hear, smell, and feel as you walk. Use your sense of taste to sample rain, snow, honeysuckles, or food growing in your garden.

I saw _____

I heard _____

I smelled _____

I felt _____

I tasted _____

3. Find a tree to observe. Look for animals and insects that may be visiting the tree. Feel and smell the bark. Observe the tree and leaf shapes. Notice the colors. Write about your tree here:

_____

_____

_____

_____

USE YOUR WORDS

There are many ways to write a nature journal. Many poets and artists have created their best work while observing nature. You may wish to write poems and stories inspired by what you see, or simply write facts and short details about your observations. There is no right or wrong way to journal, but here are some tips you may find helpful.

Learn to take field notes. Quick notes are helpful when you are observing something moving fast (such as a bird) or when you are on the go. Write any important details down quickly, without worrying about neatness or drawings.

Use descriptive words. When taking notes, describe colors, shapes, sounds, locations, and behaviors. Here's an example: Fuzzy black caterpillar, eating a green oval leaf; hot, sunny day.

Reflect. When you look back at your data and field notes, your descriptive observations will help you make new discoveries about what you are studying. Add to your notes using books and online resources to help you identify particular plants and animals and learn more about them.

Get some practice with writing in your nature journal using the following ideas.

1. Find one thing outside to describe in as much detail as possible. Can you come up with at least five words to describe it? Write them here:

_____   _____

_____   _____

_____   _____

2. Take a quick walk outside of your home. Take in as many sights and sounds as possible. Now set a timer for 1 minute and quickly write down your observations. These are your field notes.

_____

_____

_____

_____

3. Choose one plant or animal you find interesting and write an acrostic poem (a poem where the first letter of each line spells a word) about it. Make sure to use descriptive words!

Here is my example:

Busy bee

Eating nectar from flowers

Everything tastes sweet and not sour

Now it's your turn:

_____

_____

_____

_____

_____

_____

_____

PICTURE THIS

Drawing in your nature journal is a way to record colors, shapes, and features. Make sure you have fun, and don't worry about perfect drawings!

Begin with general shapes. First, sketch the overall shape of your object or nature scene.

Add in key details. Add in colors, special markings, patterns, and unique designs, and pay attention to lighting and shadows. Don't spend too much time on extra details, though, especially for quick sketches!

Keep it simple. When you are making quick field sketches, you should keep things simple. Your journal and a pencil or colored pencils are all you need.

Get creative. When you aren't in the field, you can get more creative by experimenting with additional art materials to create a more finished drawing. Felt-tip pens, watercolor paints, chalk pastels, and oil pastels are some of my favorites.

Practice. To improve your drawing skills, you will need to practice often. The more you use your skills, the better you will become.

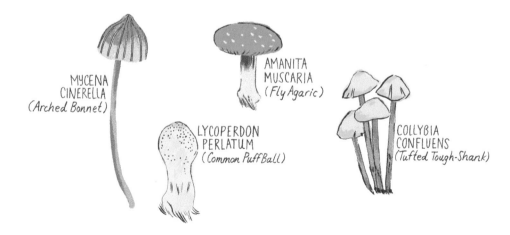

MYCENA CINERELLA (Arched Bonnet)

AMANITA MUSCARIA (Fly Agaric)

LYCOPERDON PERLATUM (Common Puff Ball)

COLLYBIA CONFLUENS (Tufted Tough-Shank)

Let's practice! Use these guidelines to sketch a mushroom.

1. Start by making a 2-inch line from left to right.

2. Add a rainbow-shape curve on top of your line.

3. Sketch a long, rounded rectangle standing up beneath your mushroom cap for the stem.

4. Add lines, details, and colors.

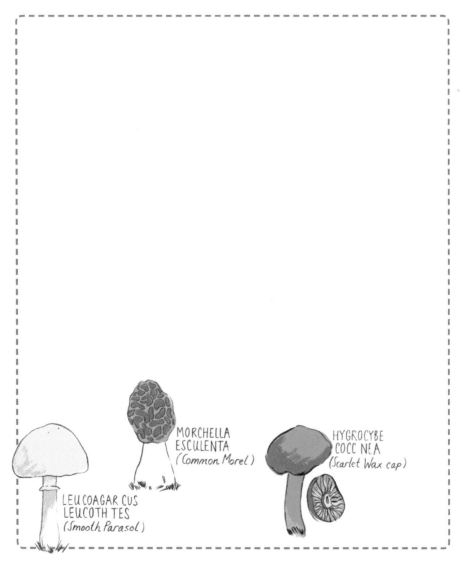

MORCHELLA
ESCULENTA
(Common Morel)

HYGROCYBE
COCC NEA
(Scarlet Wax cap)

LEUCOAGAR CUS
LEUCOTH TES
(Smooth Parasol)

THE SKY ABOVE

The sky reflects our changing seasons and the many forms of weather we experience. It also gives us the loveliness of colorful sunsets, shooting stars, constellations, cloud formations, and moon phases. The sky is full of exciting things to see!

Document the temperature and weather. Writing the temperature and weather in your journal helps you figure out what types of insects, plants, and animals thrive, or do well, in particular weather conditions. You can buy an inexpensive outdoor thermometer at most garden centers.

Use field guides. To identify clouds, moon phases, and constellations, take along guides while observing, or spend time studying them beforehand.

Plan ahead. Visit In-The-Sky.org to stay up-to-date on events happening in the night sky. Meteor showers are a must-see!

Visit the same place. One of the best ways to notice seasonal changes is to visit the same tree, garden, or other outdoor spot on a weekly basis. Observe and document new plant growth, insect and animal life, as well as seasonal colors and landscape changes.

Try these journaling activities to help you learn more about the sky and the seasons.

1. Observe the moon as many nights as you can for a month. Draw and label each night's moon phase in your journal. Is the moon waxing (getting closer to full) or waning (getting closer to a new moon)?

2. Observe the daytime sky early in the morning and then again right before sunset. Remember not to look directly at the sun! Draw what you see.

3. One way to learn what happens each season in your area is to keep a calendar of "firsts." Document these firsts in your journal while you're exploring: the first snow, first butterfly of spring, first dandelion after winter. Once you get home, copy these into a perpetual calendar (a calendar that works for many years). Over time, your calendar will be a great tool for understanding the seasonal changes of your region.

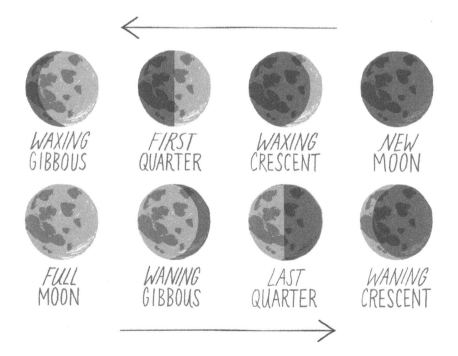

THE EARTH BELOW

The natural home of a plant, animal, or other organism is called its "habitat." Different creatures need different habitats: You find seagulls and palm trees in a coastal habitat, while camels and cactuses prefer the dry habitat of the desert. From the sand dunes on the beach to the vast greenery of the grasslands, each habitat has its own features. Here are a few tips for determining what habitat you live in.

Observe the ground. Is there sand, soil, or clay? Is it flat, hilly, or mountainous? What colors do you see?

Study the flora and fauna. Flora and fauna are the plants and animals of a habitat. Identify what's growing and what critters live nearby.

Research. With the help of books, online resources, and your observations, you will be able to identify different habitats wherever you go!

COMMON ANIMAL TRACKS

DEER	RACCOON	DOG
MOUSE	SQUIRREL	RABBIT
OPOSSUM	SKUNK	COYOTE
		F=Front TRACK H=Hind TRACK

Here are some journaling ideas to try when you travel or visit new habitats.

1. Look for sand ripples, flood-carved canyons, succulent plants and cactuses, dung beetles, and lizards if you visit the desert. Journal about your findings.

2. When at the beach, search for tide pools (shallow pools of water left after high tide). What plant and animal life are hiding inside? Draw them in your journal.

3. Visit a forest and journal about four different tree species you find there. Are the trees deciduous (have leaves drop in the fall) or coniferous (have needles and cones, and are often evergreen with a triangular shape)? Use a field guide or online sources to determine which trees you observed.

4. Hike a mountain trail and look for signs of animal life. Can you find footprints, animal scat, or claw markings on a tree? Write about your hike in your nature journal.

SCAT IDENTIFICATION CHART

DEER	RACCOON	DOG
MOUSE	SQUIRREL	RABBIT
OPOSSUM	SKUNK	COYOTE

WILD CREATURES

Wild creatures are living all around us. Sometimes they are easy to spot, but other times we have to know where to look! Here are some tips to help you get to know the animals living in your neighborhood.

Look up, under, and inside. Look up in the trees and sky. Look under rocks, logs, and leaves. Look inside ponds, streams, holes, and caves. Bring along a walking stick to help you look under and inside objects without getting too close!

Search for clues. Keep your eye out for animal scat, footprints, nibbled acorns, tooth marks, small bones, and other clues that can tell you what wildlife is living nearby.

Bring the wildlife to you. Another way to observe wildlife is by attracting animals and bugs to your own backyard. Make a bird feeder, create a toad home, plant a butterfly garden, or build an insect hotel.

Observe, describe, document, and identify. Closely observe the wildlife you find. Describe the animal's physical details and behaviors in your journal. When you return home, use this information to research and identify what you observed.

8-19-19

Practice the tips in the previous section. What did you
see? Using the space here, draw, write about, and identify
any animals you observed.

THINGS THAT GROW

As a naturalist and a noticer, you will have so many questions about the things growing around you. Let's take a look at how you can observe, describe, identify, and journal about the plants you see.

Take safety measures. The very first thing you should do when studying the plants in your area is to find out what is poisonous. Learn about dangerous plants growing around you through online research or region-specific books, or by visiting a local nature or agriculture center and talking to an expert.

Use your senses. Observing color, shape, size, smell, and texture can give you a lot of information about a plant. Remember to stay away from the dangerous plants and mushrooms you learned about!

Draw, write, identify. Draw and write details about specific plants in your journal. Use these details to search online resources, field guides, and books to help with identification.

Visit a garden. Many local gardens and arboretums have tags with species names listed. Find a garden with labels and observe the plants. You may even want to record your favorites in your journal.

Respect nature. It can be tempting to pick pretty flowers or collect unique plants to study or draw. Respect nature by collecting only what you plan to use. Pick something only when there are plenty of other similar plants growing nearby, and always leave the roots, allowing the plant to regrow. I am a little more relaxed when it comes to collecting four-leaf clovers!

Use this space to draw, write about, and identify a plant you observed in the wild.

LOOKING BACK

You have a journal page of nature drawings, notes, and questions written while on a nature outing. Now what? Now it's time to think about what you have seen, study your notes, research, and write down any further thoughts.

1. Reread your notes and decide if you have any unanswered questions about what you saw. Maybe you discovered a fuzzy caterpillar and you want to know what type it is; or perhaps you want to better understand why there was one brown-and-white speckled egg in a nest of blue eggs.

2. Answer your questions and learn more from books, field guides, and online resources, or try asking someone who specializes in that area of nature study.

3. Write your answers and finished thoughts in the "Looking Back" section of your journal.

4. After your research, you may want to look back at your nature drawings and determine if they need any touch-ups or changes. Looking in a book or online at a close-up picture of what you observed can show you extra details you missed. You may also decide to use additional materials to create a more finished piece of nature art. This is where you can get creative and make it your own.

Think about a recent nature walk.

What did you see?

What did you wonder?

What did you learn?

HOW TO USE
THIS JOURNAL

The rest of the book is where you can really get creative and have fun! Bring this journal along on your walks and outdoor adventures. In the sections provided on each journal page, you can record the date and time, your location, and the weather.

Take quick notes on what you see or experience using the "My Field Notes" section. "Looking Back" is where you might choose to write your final thoughts or answers to your own questions after you have had time to research what you observed. The "My Field Sketches" page can be used for whatever you want! You can include quick pencil sketches, colorful nature drawings, or even poems, music, or stories inspired by your experiences outside.

Try taping in bird feathers you find, or gently gluing down your favorite pressed leaves, flowers, and clovers. Your nature journal is going to be special and unique, just like you!

Hazelnuts

Sand Dollar

Needles

Feather

Shell

Echinacea

Seedpods

Part 2

YOUR NATURE JOURNAL

In this section, you will find journal pages to use on your adventures exploring in nature. Each page includes some suggestions for information to record, but there's plenty of room for notes, drawings, and your own creativity!

You can download and print additional journal pages at CallistoMediaBooks.com/ ExploringNatureJournalForKids.

DATE AND TIME ....

LOCATION ....

WEATHER ....

MY FIELD NOTES ....

....

....

....

....

....

LOOKING BACK ....

....

....

....

....

....

....

....

DATE AND TIME 9/5/2020

LOCATION At home

WEATHER Sunny

MY FIELD NOTES

Nothing

LOOKING BACK

I got stunk

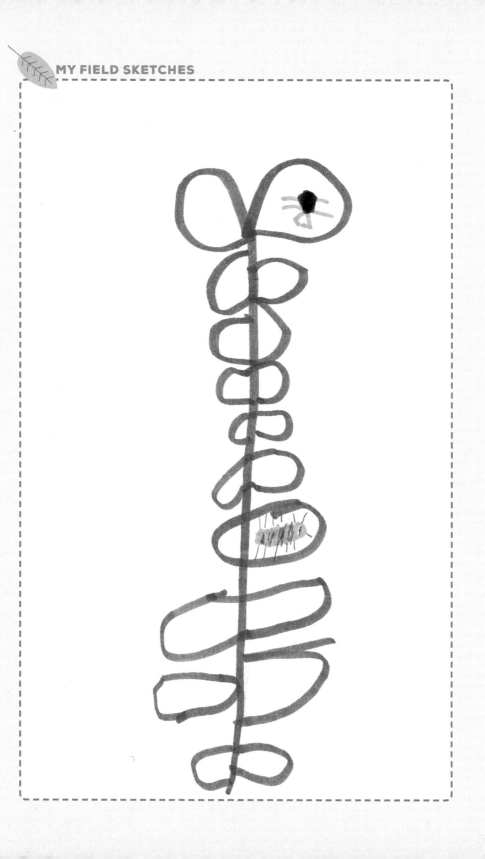

DATE AND TIME

LOCATION

WEATHER

MY FIELD NOTES

LOOKING BACK

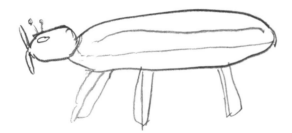

DATE AND TIME ....

LOCATION ....

WEATHER ....

MY FIELD NOTES ....

....

....

....

....

....

LOOKING BACK ....

....

....

....

....

....

....

....

....

MY FIELD SKETCHES

DATE AND TIME ....

LOCATION ....

WEATHER ....

MY FIELD NOTES ....

....

....

....

....

....

LOOKING BACK ....

....

....

....

....

....

....

....

MY FIELD SKETCHES

DATE AND TIME ....

LOCATION ....

WEATHER ....

MY FIELD NOTES ....

....

....

....

....

....

LOOKING BACK ....

....

....

....

....

....

....

....

....

DATE AND TIME ....

LOCATION ....

WEATHER ....

MY FIELD NOTES ....

....

....

....

....

....

LOOKING BACK ....

....

....

....

....

....

....

....

MY FIELD SKETCHES

DATE AND TIME ....

LOCATION ....

WEATHER ....

MY FIELD NOTES ....

....

....

....

....

....

....

LOOKING BACK ....

....

....

....

....

....

....

....

MY FIELD SKETCHES

DATE AND TIME ....

LOCATION ....

WEATHER ....

MY FIELD NOTES ....

....

....

....

....

....

....

....

LOOKING BACK ....

....

....

....

....

....

....

....

....

LOCATION

WEATHER

MY FIELD NOTES

LOOKING BACK

MY FIELD SKETCHES

DATE AND TIME

LOCATION

WEATHER

MY FIELD NOTES

LOOKING BACK

MY FIELD SKETCHES

DATE AND TIME

LOCATION

WEATHER

MY FIELD NOTES

LOOKING BACK

DATE AND TIME

LOCATION

WEATHER

MY FIELD NOTES

LOOKING BACK

DATE AND TIME ....

LOCATION ....

WEATHER ....

MY FIELD NOTES ....

....

....

....

....

....

LOOKING BACK ....

....

....

....

....

....

....

....

....

MY FIELD SKETCHES

DATE AND TIME ....

LOCATION ....

WEATHER ....

MY FIELD NOTES ....

....

....

....

....

....

LOOKING BACK ....

....

....

....

....

....

....

....

MY FIELD SKETCHES

DATE AND TIME

LOCATION

WEATHER

MY FIELD NOTES

LOOKING BACK

DATE AND TIME

LOCATION

WEATHER

MY FIELD NOTES

LOOKING BACK

MY FIELD SKETCHES

DATE AND TIME

LOCATION

WEATHER

MY FIELD NOTES

LOOKING BACK

DATE AND TIME

LOCATION

WEATHER

MY FIELD NOTES

LOOKING BACK

DATE AND TIME

LOCATION

WEATHER

MY FIELD NOTES

LOOKING BACK

DATE AND TIME

LOCATION

WEATHER

MY FIELD NOTES

LOOKING BACK

MY FIELD SKETCHES

LOCATION

WEATHER

MY FIELD NOTES

LOOKING BACK

MY FIELD SKETCHES

DATE AND TIME

LOCATION

WEATHER

MY FIELD NOTES

LOOKING BACK

DATE AND TIME

LOCATION

WEATHER

MY FIELD NOTES

LOOKING BACK

MY FIELD SKETCHES

DATE AND TIME

LOCATION

WEATHER

MY FIELD NOTES

LOOKING BACK

MY FIELD SKETCHES

DATE AND TIME

LOCATION

WEATHER

MY FIELD NOTES

LOOKING BACK

MY FIELD SKETCHES

DATE AND TIME _____

LOCATION _____

WEATHER _____

MY FIELD NOTES _____

_____

_____

_____

_____

_____

LOOKING BACK _____

_____

_____

_____

_____

_____

_____

_____

DATE AND TIME --

LOCATION --

WEATHER ---

MY FIELD NOTES --

LOOKING BACK --

MY FIELD SKETCHES

DATE AND TIME ....

LOCATION ....

WEATHER ....

MY FIELD NOTES ....

....

....

....

....

....

....

LOOKING BACK ....

....

....

....

....

....

....

....

....

MY FIELD SKETCHES

DATE AND TIME

LOCATION

WEATHER

MY FIELD NOTES

LOOKING BACK

MY FIELD SKETCHES

DATE AND TIME

LOCATION

WEATHER

MY FIELD NOTES

LOOKING BACK

DATE AND TIME ....

LOCATION ....

WEATHER ....

MY FIELD NOTES ....

....

....

....

....

....

....

LOOKING BACK ....

....

....

....

....

....

....

....

....

MY FIELD SKETCHES

DATE AND TIME --

LOCATION --

WEATHER ---

MY FIELD NOTES ---

LOOKING BACK --

DATE AND TIME ....

LOCATION ....

WEATHER ....

MY FIELD NOTES ....

....

....

....

....

....

....

LOOKING BACK ....

....

....

....

....

....

....

....

....

MY FIELD SKETCHES

About the Author

Kim Andrews is a North Carolina–based writer and blogger. She enjoys adventures by the river with her husband and their three children, is slightly obsessed with full moons, and thinks you can never have too many pet chickens. Kim studies environmental education, teaches nature classes on her family's small farm, and blogs about her passion for exploring, crafting, and outdoor learning at LearningBarefoot.com.